Map Skills for Today®

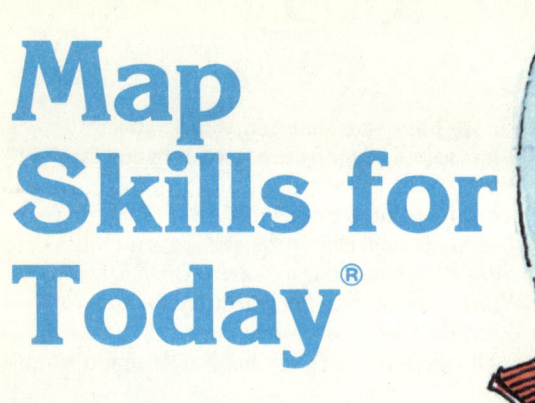

Book 2

A Weekly Reader® Skills Book

Table of Contents

What Is a Globe?	3
What Is a Map?	4
Introducing Map Symbols	5
Using Symbols	11
Introducing Boundaries	15
Introducing Directions	17
Using Symbols and Directions	18
Using Boundaries	23
Reviewing Directions and Symbols	24
Introducing the Equator	28
North America	29
United States	30
Map Skills Review—Symbols and Directions	31
Index of Skills and Understandings	32

By the Editors of *Weekly Reader®*

This book was written by Beth S. Atwood, Carolyn N. Paine, and Elaine P. Wonsavage.
Cover Art: Richard Maccabe
Publisher: Richard J. LeBrasseur

Recycled Paper

Map Skills for Today®

Map-Reading Skills Are Important

Maps are an essential tool in today's world. Everyone—the business person, the traveler, the TV news watcher—needs to know how to read maps. Maps use a unique language of symbols to show facts and relationships. Like any unfamiliar language, map language must be carefully studied to be understood.

Map Skills for Today, Book 2 is written at an average second-grade reading level. One in a series of six books, *Book 2* reviews skills from *Book 1*, introduces new terms, and offers activities that involve simple map symbols and the use of cardinal directions. A detailed list of skills and understandings can be found on page 32.

Distinctive Features of the Series

Sequential Skills Program. The series comprises a developmental program of basic map-reading skills, beginning with the relationship between a child's world and maps and progressing to the use of map scales, projections, and multiple maps.

Content Emphases. Though the goal of the series is to build compentency in map reading—vital to students whatever the curriculum—the books do reflect familiar social studies areas.

Book 1—imaginary settings, small-area maps, globes
Book 2—small-area maps, countries of North America
Book 3—regions of the United States, some individual states
Book 4—countries of the world; regions of the United States, featuring special-purpose maps
Book 5—Western Hemisphere, including the United States
Book 6—world view, using various projections and special-purpose maps; continents, regions, countries.

Review. Each book provides concise review of materials in preceding books as well as ample reinforcement of new skills.

Procedures for Using This Book

Step 1. Introduce the Topic. Before students start this book, spend some time building background to help students understand and appreciate maps.

Kinds of Maps. Guide discussion with questions such as:
- What kinds of maps have you seen?
- Where have you seen maps being used?
- What kinds of maps are used by your family?
- Why would these people need maps: an explorer, an airplane pilot, a police officer, a truck driver?

Using the Globe. Show the students a globe. Discuss the following questions to familiarize the class with the globe.
- What color stands for water on the globe?
- What do other colors stand for?
- Is the greater part of the Earth made up of land or water?
- What are the large bodies of water called?
- On what part of the globe do we live?

Using a Map. Show the students a map of the United States. Point out your state. Find the approximate position of your state on the globe. Ask the class to tell ways the map and the globe are alike and ways they are different.

Step 2. Guide the Lesson. Most students will gain more from the pages if some guidance is given, especially at the beginning. The following procedure is suggested.
- Read the title of the page.
- Discuss each map and/or illustrations. Discuss what is shown. Point out the labels on the maps.
- List on the board any new word from the page.
- Read and discuss the introduction with the students. Read the directions together.
- Begin by working orally through a whole page with the class. After working several pages in this manner, students may work independently—with guidance through the first exercise on each page.

Step 3. Have Students Work Independently. Be sure students understand directions before they work independently. Caution students to follow directions and to study maps very carefully.

Step 4. Evaluate Students' Work. Check answers the students have given for the exercises, using the key provided with your classroom order of this book. Discuss students' answers and their reasons for giving them.

Step 5. Extend the Learning. Provide activities to enrich, expand, and clarify learning of map skills.
- Introduce maps of local interest.
- Help students draw maps of their homes, the school and grounds, the neighborhood.
- Have a treasure hunt, using a map of the classroom or other area of the school.

Copyright © 1986 by Weekly Reader Corporation. All rights reserved. *Weekly Reader* and *Map Skills for Today* are federally registered trademarks of Weekly Reader Corporation. Publishing, Executive, and Editorial Offices: 200 First Stamford Place, Stamford, CT 06912-0023. Subscription Offices: 3001 Cindel Drive, Delran, NJ 08370; 1-800-446-3355. Printed in U.S.A. Material in this book may not be reproduced; stored in a retrieval system; or transmitted in any form or by any means, electronic, mechanical, photocopying, or other, without special permission from the publisher.

17/98 97

ISBN: 0-8374-0224-7

What Is a Globe?

Dear Mapmaker,
   I would like to find out more about globes. Please tell me some things I should know about globes.
         Yours truly,
   Tommy Trip

Dear Tommy,
   The Earth is very large. We can see only a small part of it at a time. Even a picture taken from an airplane shows only a tiny part of the whole Earth.

   A globe is a small model of the Earth. A globe is round because the Earth looks round.

   Here are some of the things you need to know before using globes and maps.

   Continents and Oceans. The Earth's largest land areas are *continents*. The largest water areas are *oceans*.

   Directions. *North* is the direction toward the North Pole. *South* is the direction toward the South Pole.

   Up and Down. Up is the direction away from the center of the Earth. Down is the direction toward the center of the Earth.
         Yours truly,
   Mapmaker

North America

What Is a Map?

A map is a drawing that can show all or part of the Earth. A globe is more like the Earth. But sometimes a map can be more useful than a globe.

A globe must be turned to see the whole Earth. A map can show the whole Earth at once. A map can show small parts of the Earth larger and make them easier to see.

You can see the continent of North America on Tommy's globe on page 3 and on the map above. A map may show smaller parts of land and water better than a globe. The shapes of countries are easier to see on some maps.

Map Reading

On the map, find three oceans. Find Canada, Mexico, and the United States. Color in the parts of the United States that are shown. (Hawaii is not shown on this map.)

Map Symbols

Mapmakers use special marks and lines to stand for real things. These special marks are called **symbols.** To read maps, you should know some map symbols.

Two symbols are shown on this page. Both symbols stand for water. The color blue often stands for water.

A **river** is water that flows in one direction. Look at the photo of the river. Then read the symbol for river.

A **lake** is water with land all around it. Look at the photo of the lake. Then read the symbol for lake.

Map Symbols

Circle each place which would usually be shown as a blue symbol on a map.

lake   ocean

brook   continent

country   river

The name of a lake or river is often written by that symbol on a map. By each symbol below, write the name of a lake or river near your home.

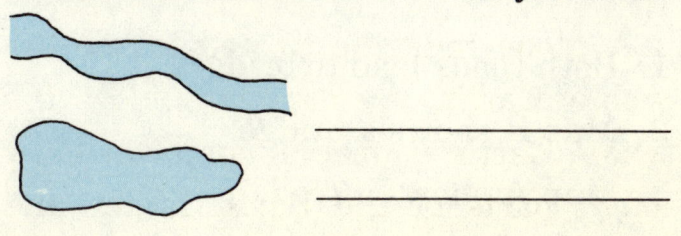

5

Map Symbols

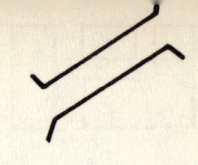

The symbols shown on this page stand for things that people have built. What other things besides bridges and highways are made by people?

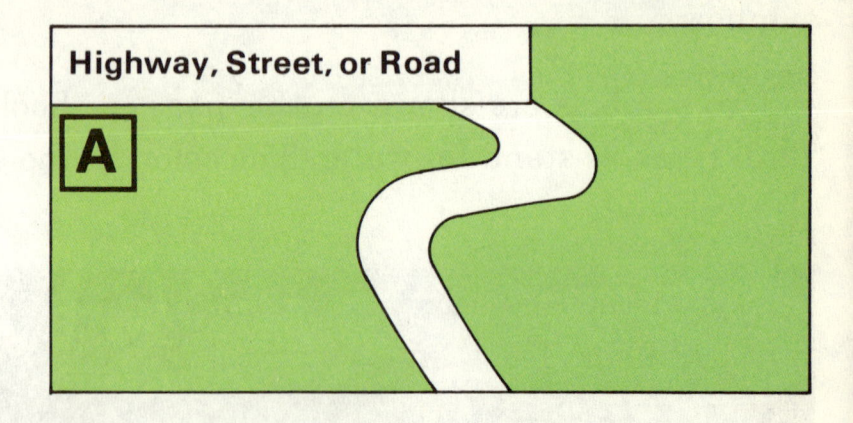

Highway, Street, or Road

A

Bridge

B

Look at each photo. Read the symbol for a highway, street, or road. Read the symbol for a bridge. What other symbol is used on the maps?

Map Reading

Underline each sentence that is true according to *these* maps.

1. Both roads lead to bridges.
2. Map **B** shows a bridge.
3. Map **A** shows a road.
4. Both maps show water.
5. Highways, streets, and roads are shown by the same symbol.
6. Land is shown by the color blue.

What kind of bridge is Tommy using?

Map Symbols

Many kinds of symbols show buildings and trees. Buildings can be drawn to look just as they are. Or buildings can be shown as small boxes. It is easier to use small boxes on a city map.

Look at the photo of a city. Find the twin buildings. Then, find **A** on the map. The two gold shapes are a symbol for the buildings.

Find buildings **B** and **C** on the photo.

Which symbol stands for a tree? Draw it in this space.

Map Reading

Circle the words that show things made by people on the map.

| bridges | lake | streets |
| buildings | trees | river |

Underline each true sentence.

1. Three bridges cross the river.
2. Buildings **A** are taller than Building **B**.
3. There are trees in the park where the two rivers meet.
4. Bridge 2 is longer than Bridge 1.

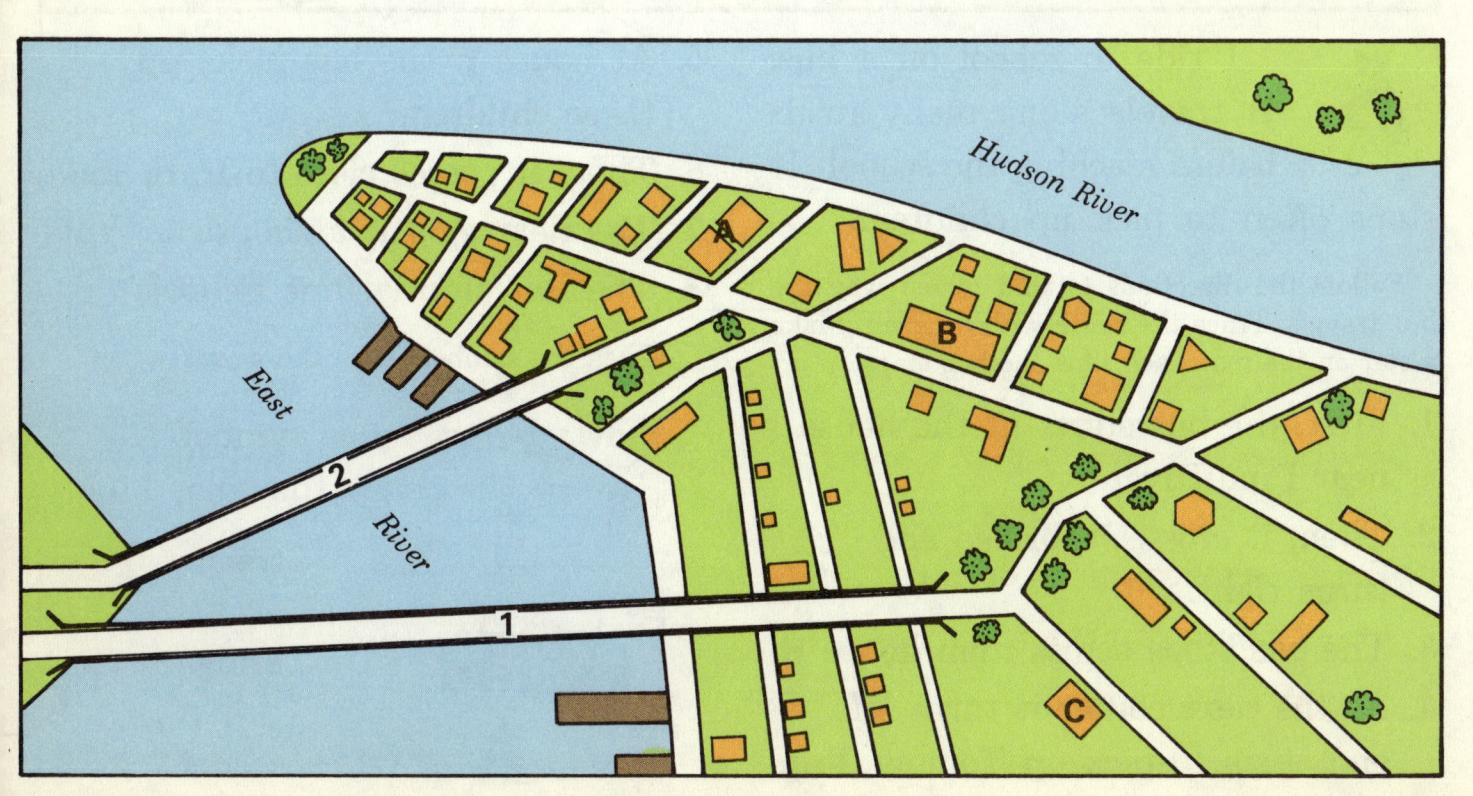

Tommy's Route to School

I ride to school on a bus. It travels along many roads before reaching the school. It stops often to pick up children.

Follow the directions to find which way the bus travels. Trace the route with a pencil. Make a star on the map each time the bus stops.

1. First, the bus starts at the house near Pine River.
2. Then, it crosses a bridge and turns right.
3. The bus stops across from house **H**.
4. At the next corner it turns left, and stops to pick up Tommy Trip.
5. At house **T**, the bus picks up three children.
6. Then, it passes close to Dark Lake.
7. The next stop is at house **D**.
8. The last stop is Pine School.

Match the symbols with the words.

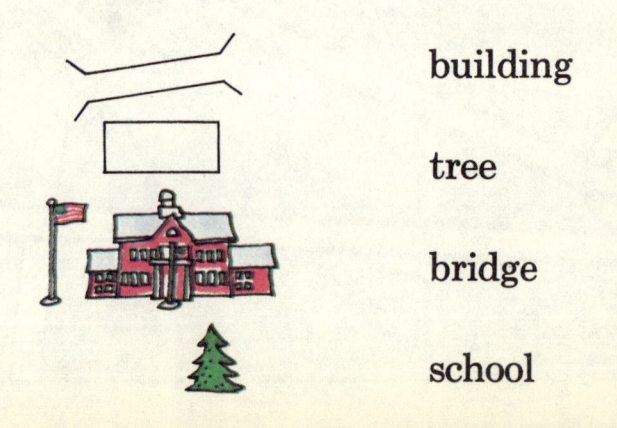

building

tree

bridge

school

8

Map Symbols

The top photo shows mountains and hills. The mountains are steep and high. The tops, or peaks, are pointed. The hills are lower, smoother, and less steep. However, not all hills and mountains are the same shape as those shown in the top photo.

The bottom photo shows a train going through mountain country. How are the mountains in this photo different from those in the top photo?

Read the symbol chart. If you made a map of both photos, would you use the same symbols on each map? Why?

Using Symbols

Circle the symbols you would need to use on a map of the bottom photo.

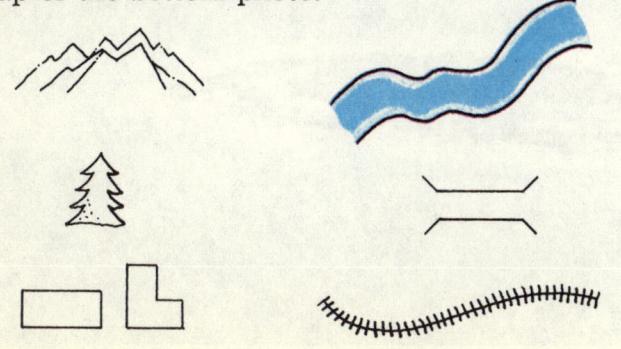

Circle the word or group of words that *best* completes each sentence.

1. Lake and mountain symbols are needed for a map of the ....

    top photo   bottom photo

2. The symbol for railroad looks like a real ....

    train   engine   track

Map Symbols

An island is land surrounded by water. Islands can be many different shapes and sizes. There are islands in rivers, lakes, and oceans. Find the islands on the map. What are their names? What ocean are they in?

Can you tell if the boys camp is on an island? Why or why not?

I've found the best place to fish. I rowed from camp to the little island between Pine Island and Hook Island. Mark the spot on your map so you can remember which island it is.

Map Reading

Circle the things you can find on the map.

river   railroad
trees   buildings
ocean   islands
bridge   names

Underline each true sentence.

1. There are trees on Hook Island.
2. The boys camp is on Hook Island.
3. There are buildings on Pine Island.
4. Ring Island is closer to Pine Island than to Hook Island.
5. Hook Island is the largest island.
6. All the islands are named.
7. The boys camp is near the water.

Tommy's Vacation Trip

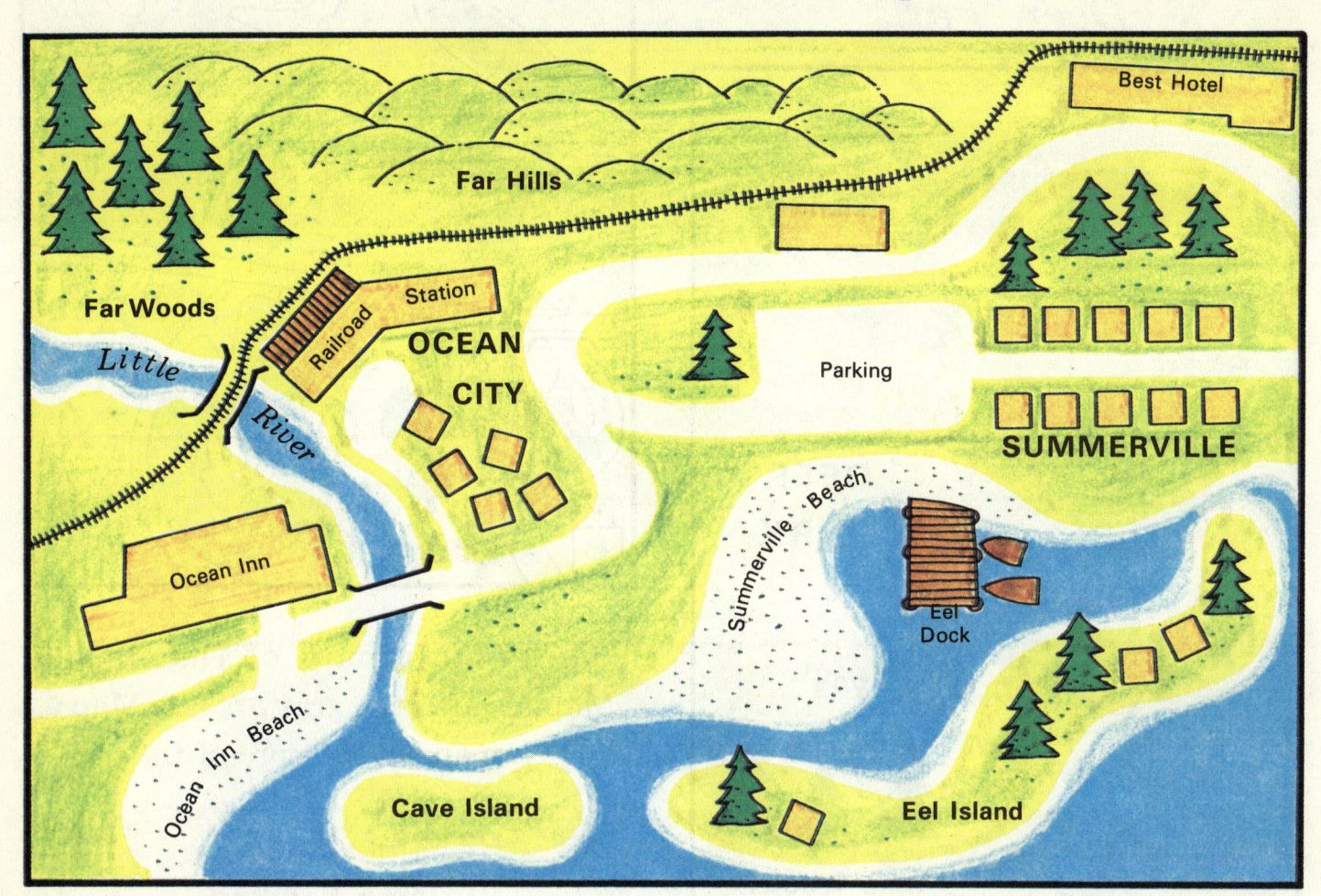

Dear Mapmaker,

I am going to Summerville for a week's vacation at the ocean. Please make a map I can use while I am there.

        Yours truly,

Tommy Trip

Dear Tommy,

On this map of Summerville you will find many symbols you already know. The names of other places have been written on the map.

        Yours truly,

Mapmaker

Map Reading

Underline each true sentence.

1. Buildings are shown on Cave Island.
2. Ocean Inn has its own beach.
3. Summerville is on Eel Island.
4. Visitors to Summerville might use the beach near Eel Dock.
5. Far Hills is next to the ocean.

Taking a Trip

Under each bold-faced word, circle the places Tommy could go to by a car, a train, or a boat.

car	train	boat
Ocean Inn	Ocean City	Far Hills
Summerville	Eel Island	Cave Island
Far Woods	Summerville	Far Woods

Deer Park

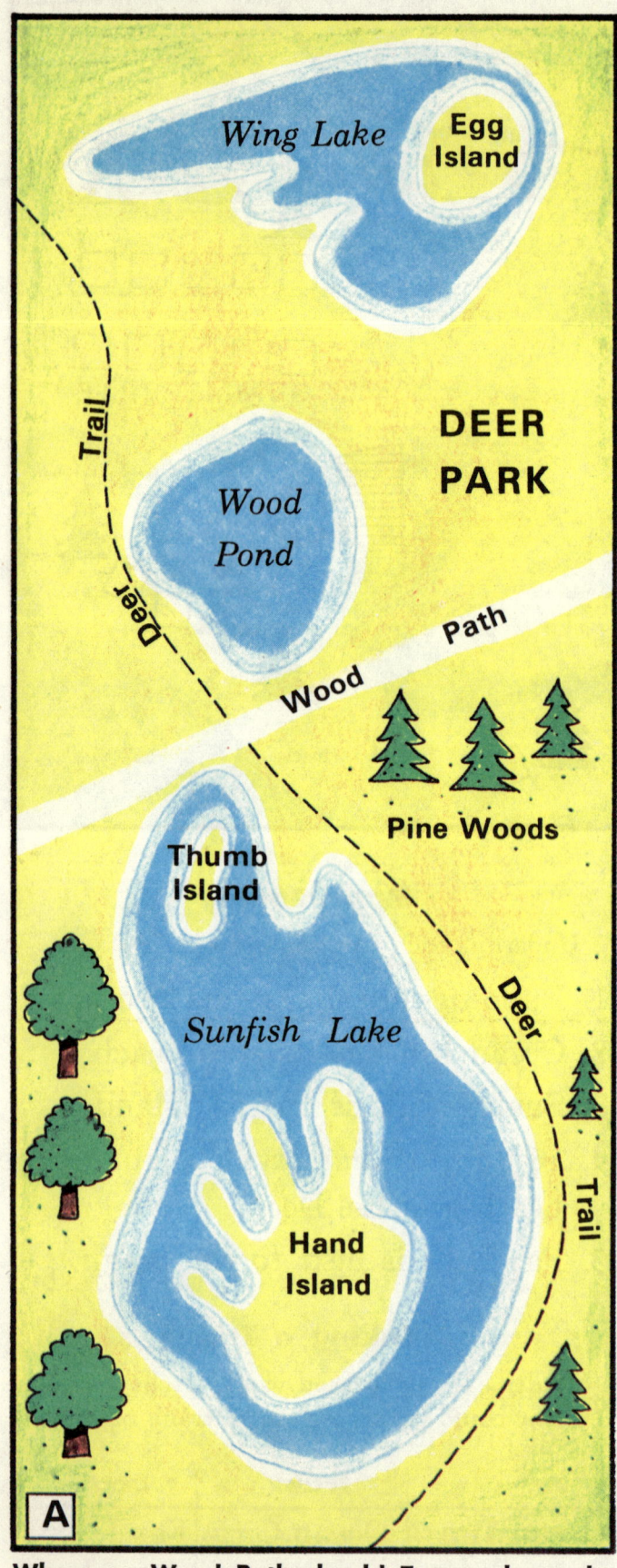

Where on Wood Path should Tommy have the best chance of seeing a deer? Make a red X at that point.

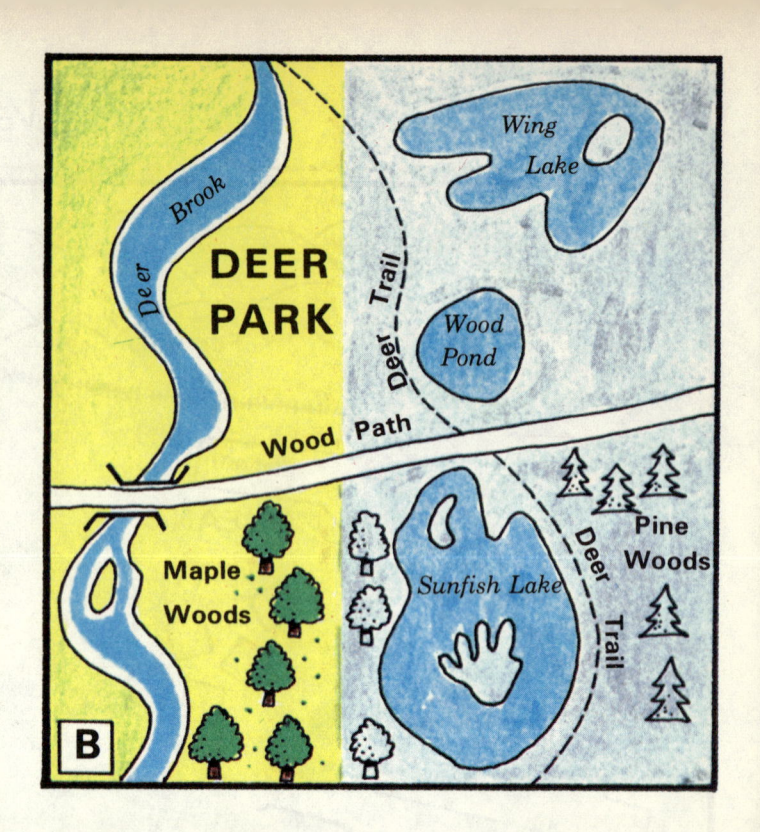

Read both maps of Deer Park. Map **A** shows the gray area on Map **B**. Which map shows more of the park?

Map Reading

Which map would you use to find the facts below? Match the columns. You will use some map names more than once.

1. Name of an island   Map B
2. A bridge
3. Names of the lakes   Both maps
4. Name of a brook
5. Names of the woods   Map A

How Big? How Small?

Underline each true sentence.

1. Hand Island is larger than Thumb Island.
2. Wing Lake is smaller than Wood Pond.
3. Egg Island is the largest island.

A Visit to Lazy Lake

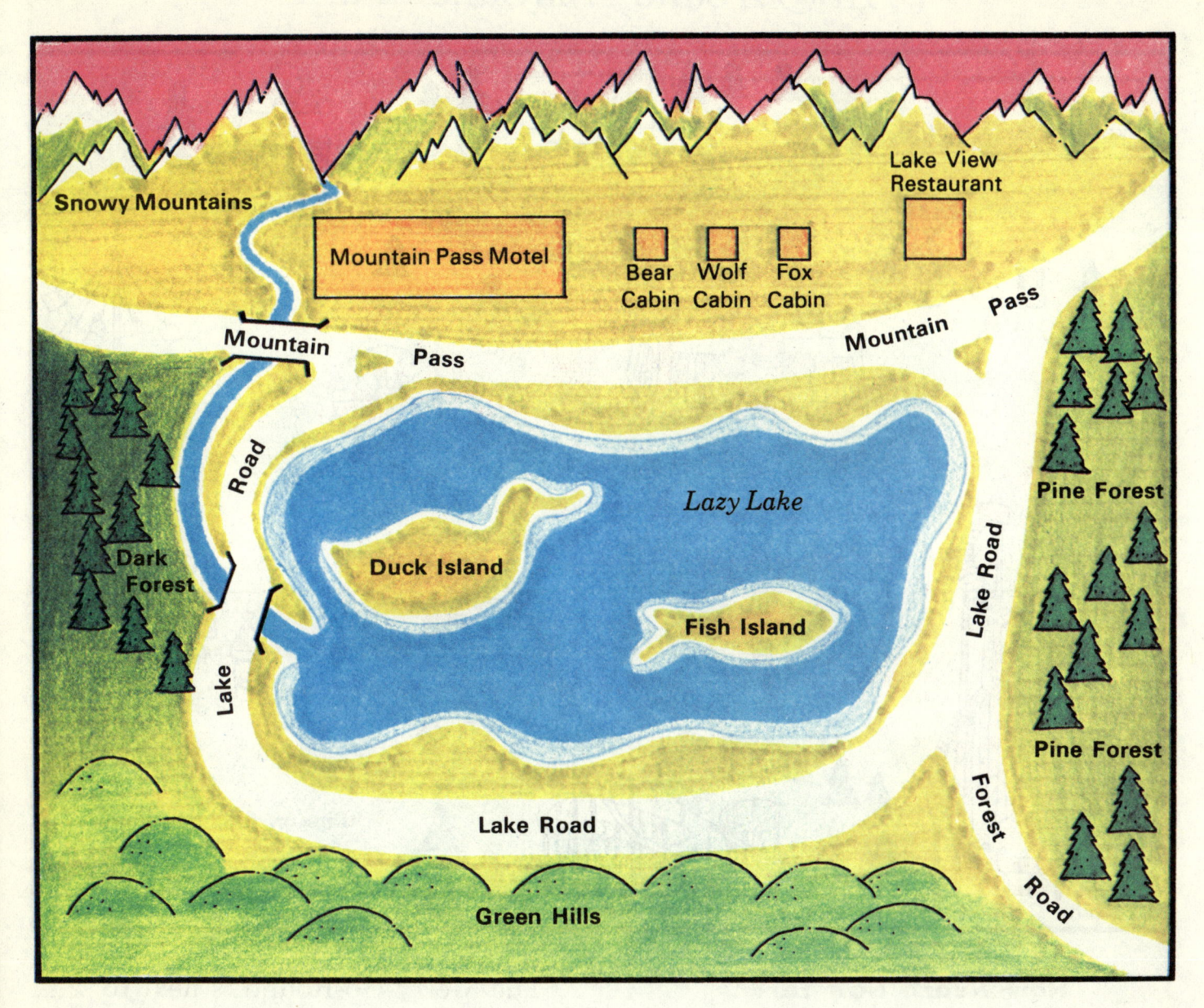

How Big? How Small?

Underline each true sentence.

1. Mountain Pass Motel is larger than Lake View Restaurant.
2. Fish Island is larger than Duck Island.
3. On the map, Pine Forest is smaller than Dark Forest.
4. Snowy Mountains are higher than the Green Hills.
5. Lake View Restaurant is larger than Fox Cabin.

Where Does the Road Go?

Circle the group of words that *best* completes each sentence.

1. Forest Road goes by ....
   Dark Forest   Pine Forest
       Snowy Mountains

2. Lake Road goes .... Lazy Lake.
   all around   away from
         partly around

3. Mountain Pass goes ....
   near Green Hills   over a bridge
         across Fish Island

13

All Around Playland Park

How Near? How Far?

Circle all the places below that are *nearer* to Gate 1 than to Gate 2.

Fun House	Merry-Go-Round
Boat Ride	Roller Coaster
Rocket Ride	Picnic Grounds
Lake Walk	Shiny Lake

Circle the word or group of words that *best* completes each sentence.

1. The shortest way to go from Gate 1 to the Picnic Grounds is by ....
   Lake Walk   Circle Lane   Park Road

2. The Merry-Go-Round is next to ....
   Swings   Fun House   Gate 1

3. The nearest place to Pine Woods Parking Lot is ....
   Boat Ride   Picnic Grounds   Swings

Map Study

Underline each true sentence.

1. The parking lots are the same size.
2. Fun House is the largest building.
3. There are trees near the lake.
4. Fun House is near Park Road.
5. A bridge crosses Shiny Lake.

From the Farm to the Village

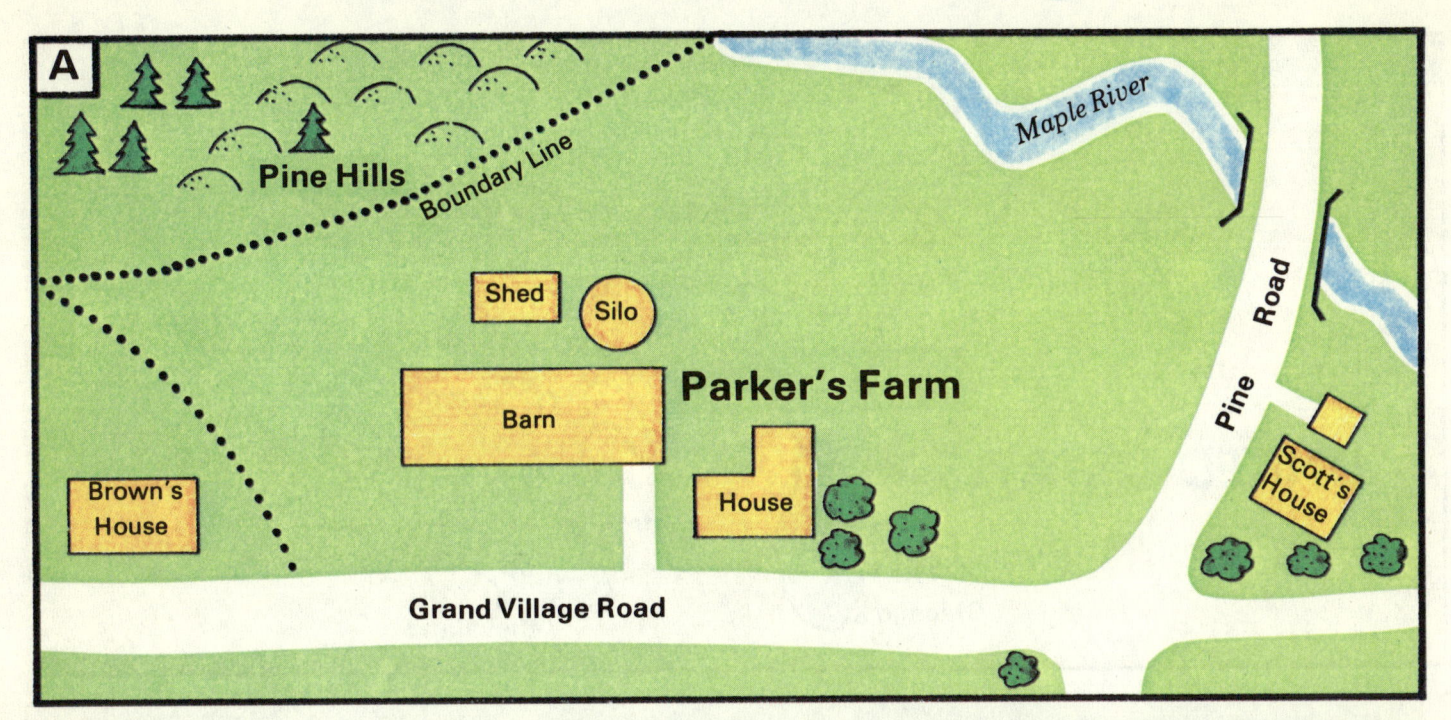

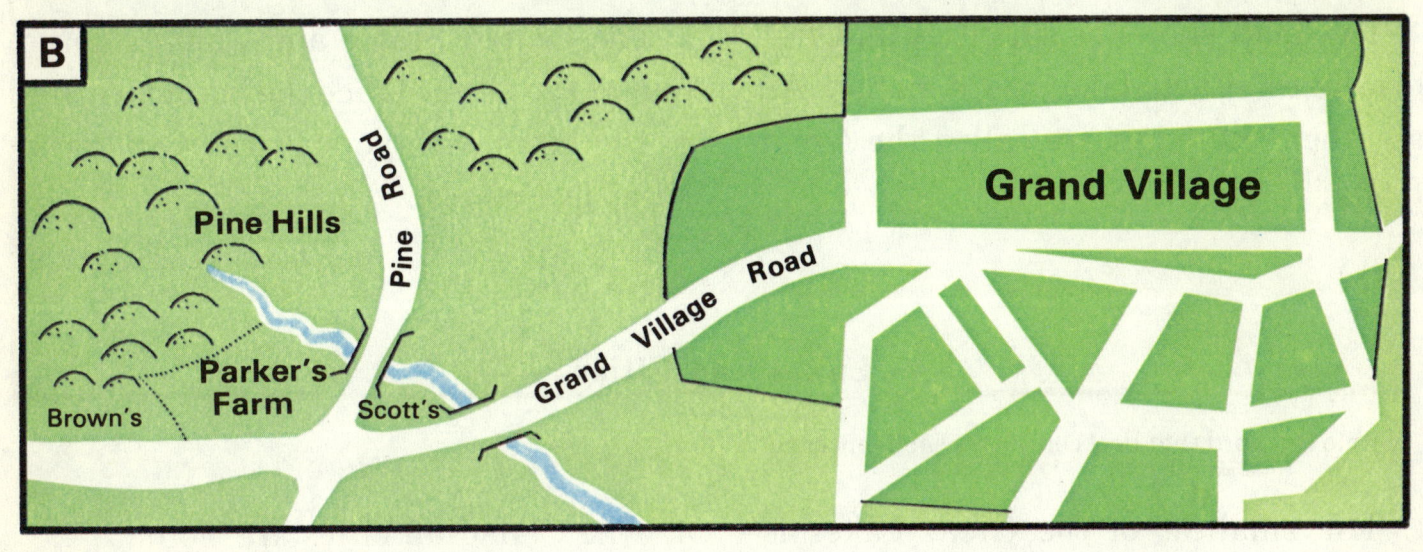

Map A shows Parker's Farm. The map shows which land belongs to the Parkers. The line where the Parkers' land ends is a boundary line. Part of the boundary line is shown by a dotted line. Roads and rivers may also be boundaries.

Map B shows more of the land around Parker's Farm. The map shows a nearby village. How are the boundary lines of the village shown?

Map Study

Underline each true sentence.

1. Scott's house is on Pine Road.
2. The shed is larger than the barn.
3. The road in front of Brown's house goes into Grand Village.
4. Maple River looks wider on Map B than on Map A.
5. Map A shows trees and buildings.

The Great Lakes

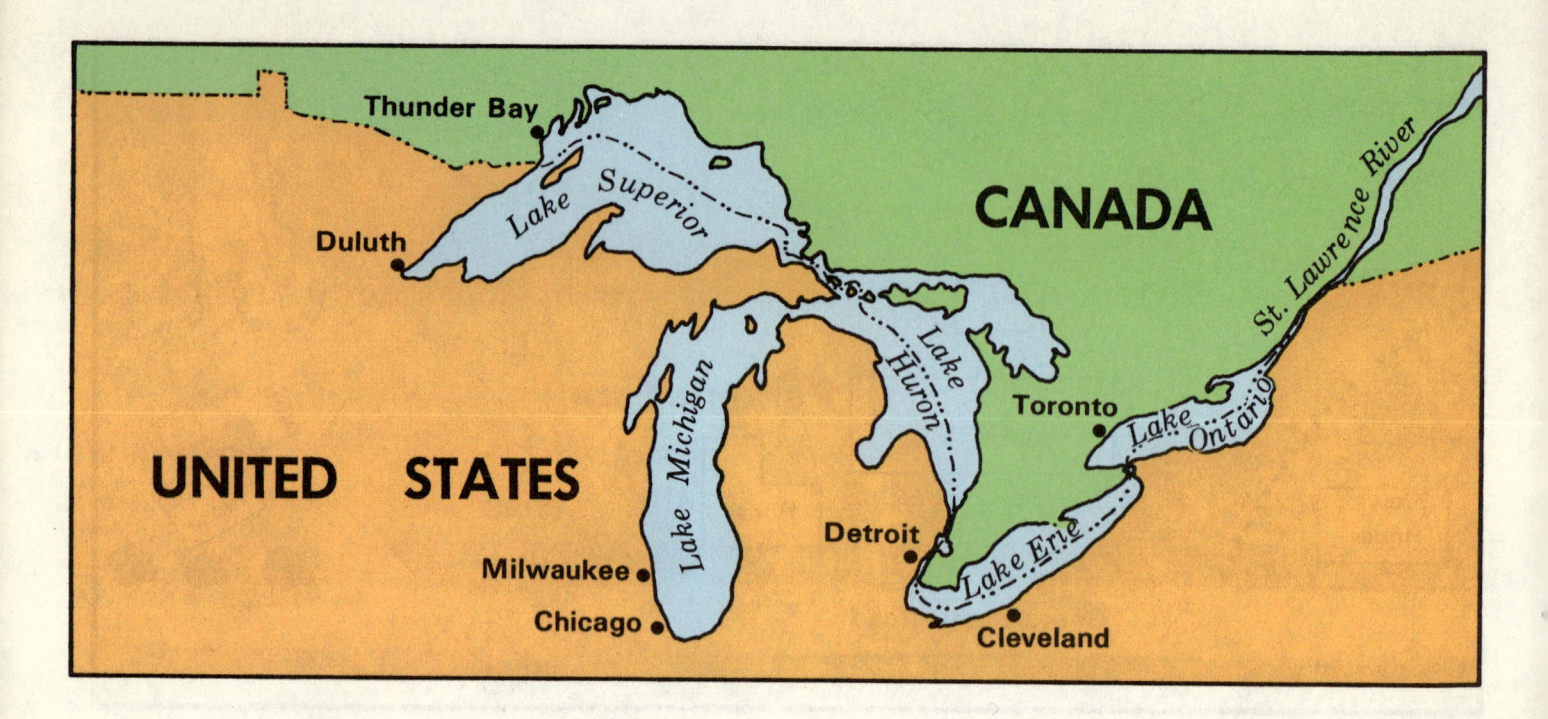

The map shows seven cities and five big lakes. Each lake has a name. All together, the lakes are called the *Great Lakes*.

The United States and Canada share four of the lakes. Trace the boundary line in the lakes with your finger. Circle the cities in Canada.

Lakes and Cities

Circle the word that best completes each sentence.

1. The smallest of the Great Lakes is Lake _____.
   Erie   Ontario   Huron

2. Canada shares every lake except Lake _____.
   Michigan   Superior   Erie

3. The map does not show a city on Lake _____.
   Ontario   Michigan   Huron

4. The Canadian cities are Toronto and _____.
   Detroit   Thunder Bay   Milwaukee

5. The city closest to Detroit is _____.
   Cleveland   Toronto   Duluth

6. The largest island is in Lake _____.
   Huron   Michigan   Superior

Find Tommy's Lost Dog

Finding Directions

Face north. South is behind you. East is to your right. → West is to your left. ← Look at the map of the field below. The directions *north*, *south*, *east*, and *west* are marked on the map. Use these directions to find Tommy's dog.

Once Tommy's dog chased a rabbit. Tommy ran after his dog. Draw a line to show where Tommy's dog and the rabbit went. The directions in the sentences tell you where to draw your lines.

1. The dog chased the rabbit *east* into the garden.
2. The rabbit hopped *south* to the log.
3. The dog chased the rabbit *west* to the pine tree.
4. The rabbit ran *south* to the bushes.
5. The dog followed the rabbit *east* to the tall grass.
6. The rabbit hopped *north* to the pond.
7. The dog chased the rabbit *east* to the stone.
8. The rabbit ran *south* to the stump and popped down a hole.
9. The dog ran to the stump, then *west* to the tall grass to meet Tommy.

Visit the Zoo

Using Directions

Find the words *north*, *south*, *east*, *west* on this map. Then find the animals on the *east* side of the zoo.

In the list below, circle the names of the animals that are *east* of Zoo Street.

Tiger	Elephant	Lion
Bears	Goats	Seals
Monkeys	Alligator	Sheep
Zebra	Giraffes	Birds

Using the Map

Underline each true sentence.

1. Alligator Alley is north of Monkey Lane.
2. Zebra Way goes north and south.
3. Short Way is east of Wildcat Walk.
4. Monkey Lane goes east and west.
5. The tiger is west of Zoo Street.
6. More streets go north and south than east and west.

Tommy Visits Bar Z Ranch

Using Directions

Use words from this list to complete the sentences: *north, south, east, west.*

1. Range Road is _____ of Bar Z Range.
2. Rope River goes mostly _____ and _____ .
3. The ranch house is _____ of the river.
4. The mountains are _____ of the railroad.
5. Lucky Lake is _____ of the Ten Hills.
6. Ox Road goes _____ and _____ .

How Far? How Big?

Underline each true sentence.

1. The lake is farther from the barn than from the ranch house.
2. Deep Pond is smaller than Lucky Lake.
3. Cattle on Bar Z Range are closer to the railroad than to the horses.
4. On the map, the railroad is longer than Ox Road.

Visiting Frontier Town

Dear Girls and Boys,

I visited Frontier Town on my vacation. Frontier Town is built like a town in the days of the Old West.

Here is a map of the town.

Yours truly,

Tommy Trip

Using the Map

Circle the word or group of words that *best* answers each question.

1. Which of these is largest?
   church   school   hotel
2. Which of these is nearest the town?
   silver mine   mountains   hills
3. Traveling by roads and streets, which is farthest from the mine?
   church   sheriff's office   hills
4. Which is nearest the school?
   horse barn   hotel   pony express
5. Which is longest on the map?
   Main Street   Indian Pass Road   Nugget Street

Which Direction?

Underline each true sentence.

1. Main Street goes east and west.
2. Nugget Hotel is east of the school.
3. The church is south of Main Street.
4. The mountains are north of town.
5. Main Street goes along the south side of the sheriff's office.
6. The general store is farthest north of all the buildings.
7. Walking from the general store to the bank, you would go south.
8. The barn is west of Nugget Street.

Visiting New Town

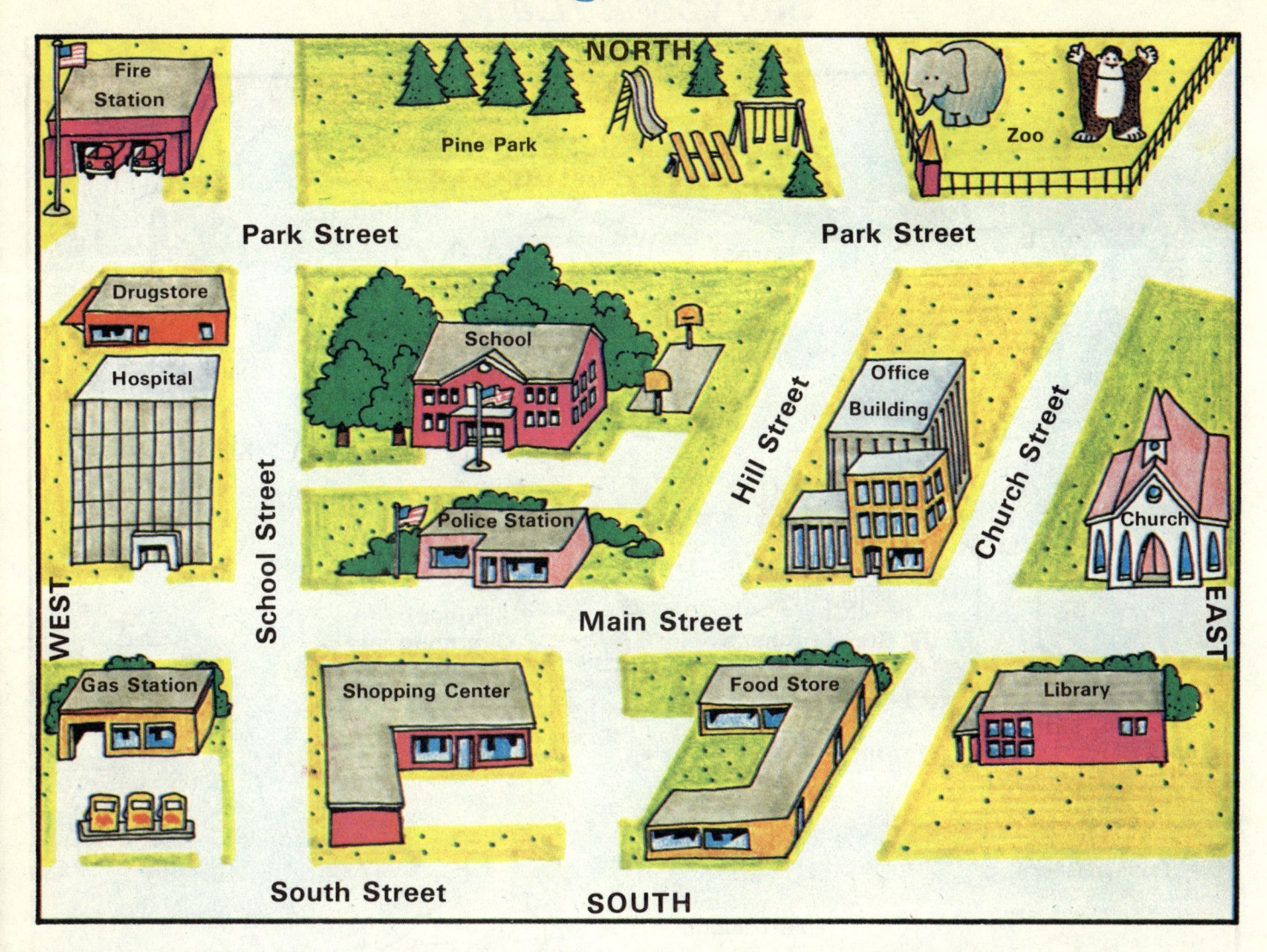

Look at the map of New Town. How is this town different from Frontier Town? What buildings do you find in New Town, but not in Frontier Town?

Using the Map

Follow the directions in each sentence.

1. Mark the shortest way to drive from the school to the library.
2. Draw a circle around the building west of the shopping center.
3. Draw a picnic table on the western side of Pine Park.
4. Draw a small building south of the zoo.
5. Mark the shortest way to drive from the zoo to the police station.
6. Circle the name of a street that goes east and west.

Reviewing Directions

Use these words to complete the sentences below: *north, south, east, west.*

1. From the shopping center to the food store, you go _____ .
2. The zoo is _____ of Park Street.
3. From the hospital to the gas station, you go _____ .
4. The fire station is _____ of the drugstore.

Storybook Land

Reviewing Directions

In the list below, circle the names of the streets which go *east and west*.

Wolf Lane	Witch's Way
Ocean Road	Castle Road
Brook Road	Forest Road

Complete the sentences by choosing a word from this list: *north, east, south, west*.

1. The witch's house is _____ of Witch's Way.
2. Grandmother's house is _____ of Heart Island.
3. Wolf Lane goes _____ and _____ .
4. The Forest Road Bridge is _____ of the castle.

Map Reading

Underline each true sentence.

1. Boots Brook flows under four bridges.
2. The ship is closer to Heart Island than the whale is.
3. Prince Charming is closer to the King's Castle than the coach is.
4. The witch's house is larger than Grandmother's house.

Camping at Porter's Pond

The light green part of the map is a camp. All the camp's boundaries are shown. Find the boundaries. Which of the boundaries is straight?

Reviewing Boundaries

Complete these sentences by choosing a word from the Word Bank. Use a word only once.

1. The lines where the camp's land ends are _____ lines.
2. Three of the camp's boundaries are made by _____.
3. The camp has _____ boundaries.
4. The camp's *west* boundary is a _____.
5. The camp's *north* boundary is a _____.
6. The camp's *east* boundary is a _____.
7. The camp's *south* boundary is a _____.

Word Bank: path, trees, brook, highway, pond, land, water, five, river, boundary, four, fence

Follow Wagon-Train Trail

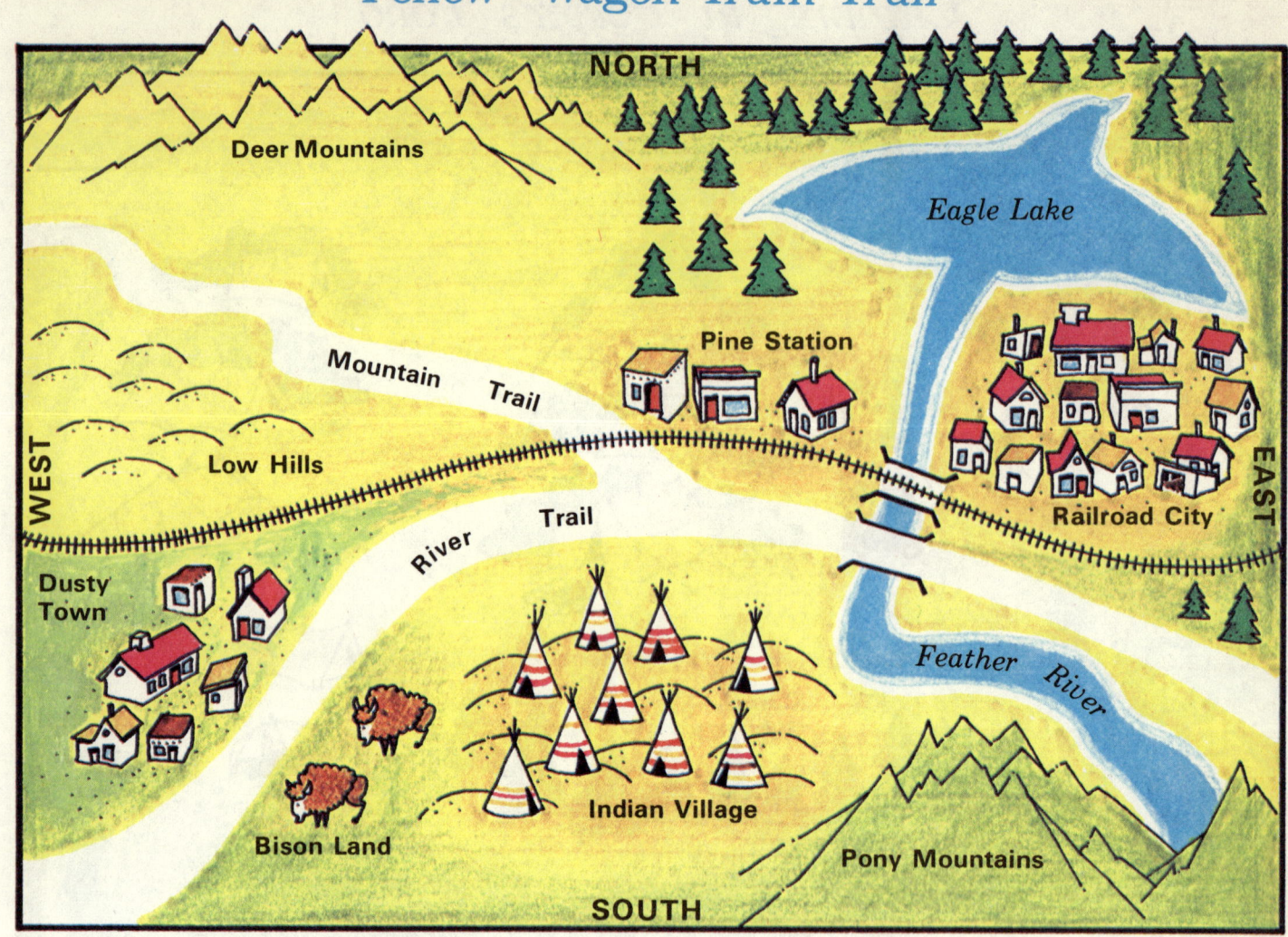

Dear Girls and Boys,

I like to read stories about the days of the Old West. I like to read about the wagon trains that went West through wild country. My map shows trails to the West.

Yours truly,

Tommy

What Does the Map Show?

Circle words that show things on the map above.

buildings	ocean
mountains	railroad
island	river
hills	bridge

Circle the word or group of words that *best* completes each sentence.

1. The railroad crosses ....
   River Trail   Feather River
   Deer Mountains

2. The Low Hills are nearest the ....
   city   railroad   lake

3. Dusty Town is larger than ....
   Railroad City   Pine Station
   Indian Village

4. The Pony Mountains are ....
   of the railroad bridge.
   south   west   north

5. Bison Land is ....
   of Indian Village.
   north   west   east

Find the Buried Treasure

Once Tommy found a note about a pirate's buried treasure. He set out to find it.

Help Tommy find the treasure by following the directions below. Draw a line to show where Tommy went. Mark an X on the map at the beginning and at the end of the line.

1. Tommy found the note in the chest *south* of Pirate Lake.
2. The note told him to cross the bridge and follow Treasure Road through the hills.
3. Then, he walked *north* to the old house. He found a new note.
4. It told him to take the road to the tree *west* of Pirate Cave.
5. He went *north* to Black Mountains, then *east* to the three trees.
6. Tommy used a boat to sail *south* to Crow Island.
7. Under the little tree he found the last note.
8. It told him to sail to the island *closest* to the Old Oak Tree.
9. The note told him to dig under the palm tree. Tommy found a pot of gold.

25

Over the Dark Mountains

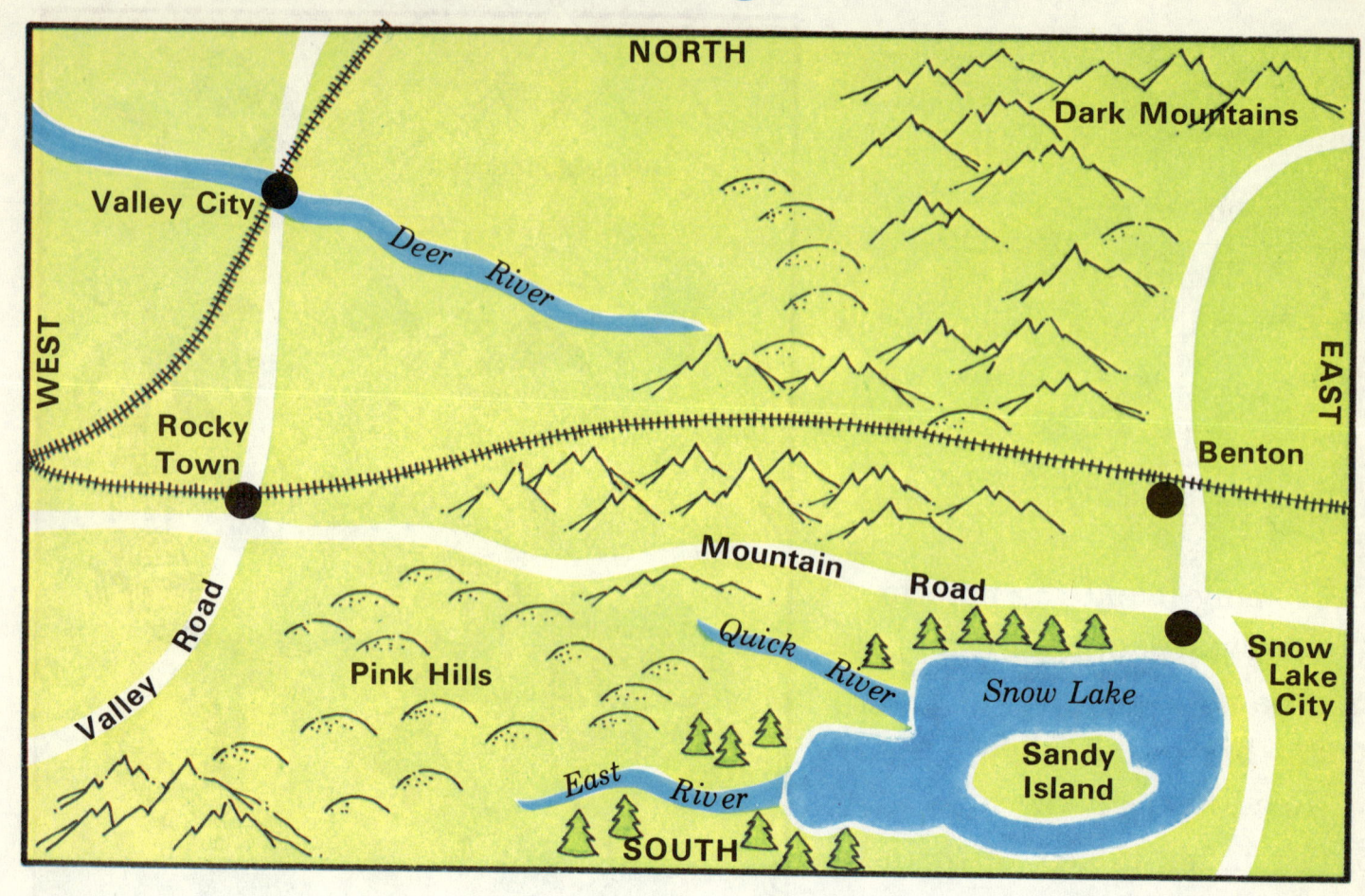

Map Study

Use the map. Then circle the things people made.

Sandy Island
Valley Road
Rocky Town
Pink Hills
Valley City
Deer River
Mountain Road
Dark Mountains

Use these words to complete the sentences: *north, south, east, west.*

1. Snow Lake is _____ of Pink Hills.
2. To go from East River to Sandy Island, you must go _____ .
3. Benton is _____ of Snow Lake City.
4. Rocky Town is _____ of Valley City.
5. From Benton to Rocky Town, trains go _____ .
6. Valley Road is _____ of the Dark Mountains.

Underline each sentence that tells something you can learn from *this* map.

1. Rocky Town is nearer to Valley City than to Benton.
2. Ten bridges cross Deer River.
3. Snow Lake City has more buildings than Rocky Town.
4. A railroad crosses the mountains.
5. Sandy Island is near the southern side of Snow Lake.
6. Deer River is longer than East River.
7. Valley City is near an ocean.

Crater Lake National Park

Map **A** and Map **B** show the same national park, Crater Lake. Which map shows cities near the park? Which one would you use while exploring the park?

Map Reading

Read Map **A**. Then underline each true sentence.

1. The park has five entrances.
2. Rim Drive goes around the lake.
3. Wizard Island is in the eastern part of the lake.
4. Most of the creeks are in the southern half of the park.
5. Sun Creek is west of the lake.
6. The buildings are mostly south of Crater Lake.
7. Grouse Hill is closer to the *north* entrance than to the *east* entrance.

Read both maps. Then complete the sentences below, using words from this list: *north, east, south, west.*

1. Driving from *Diamond Lake* to the park, you would use the _____ entrance.
2. Driving from *Canyonville* or *Medford*, you would use the _____ entrance.
3. Driving from *Klamath Falls* or *Upper Klamath Lake*, you could use the _____ entrance or the _____ entrance.

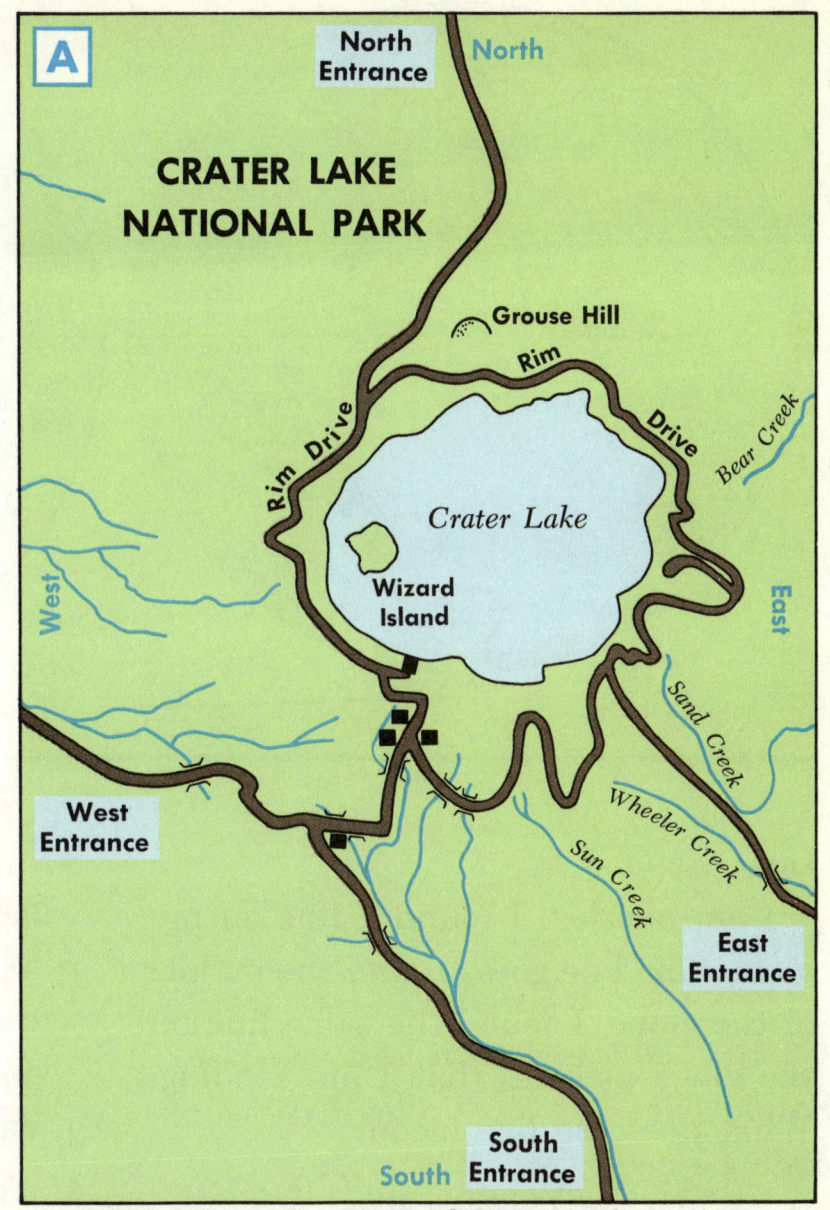

Crater Lake is the deepest lake in North America.

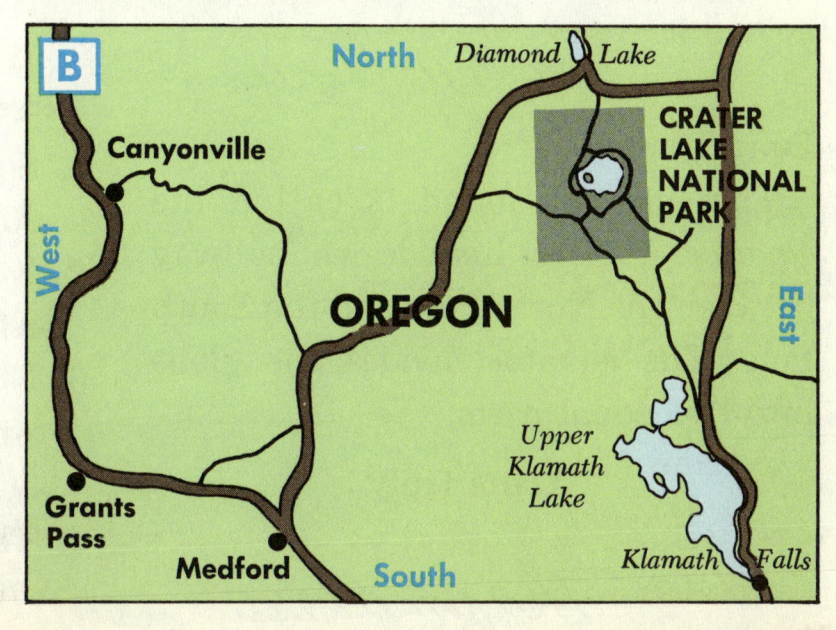

What is the Equator?

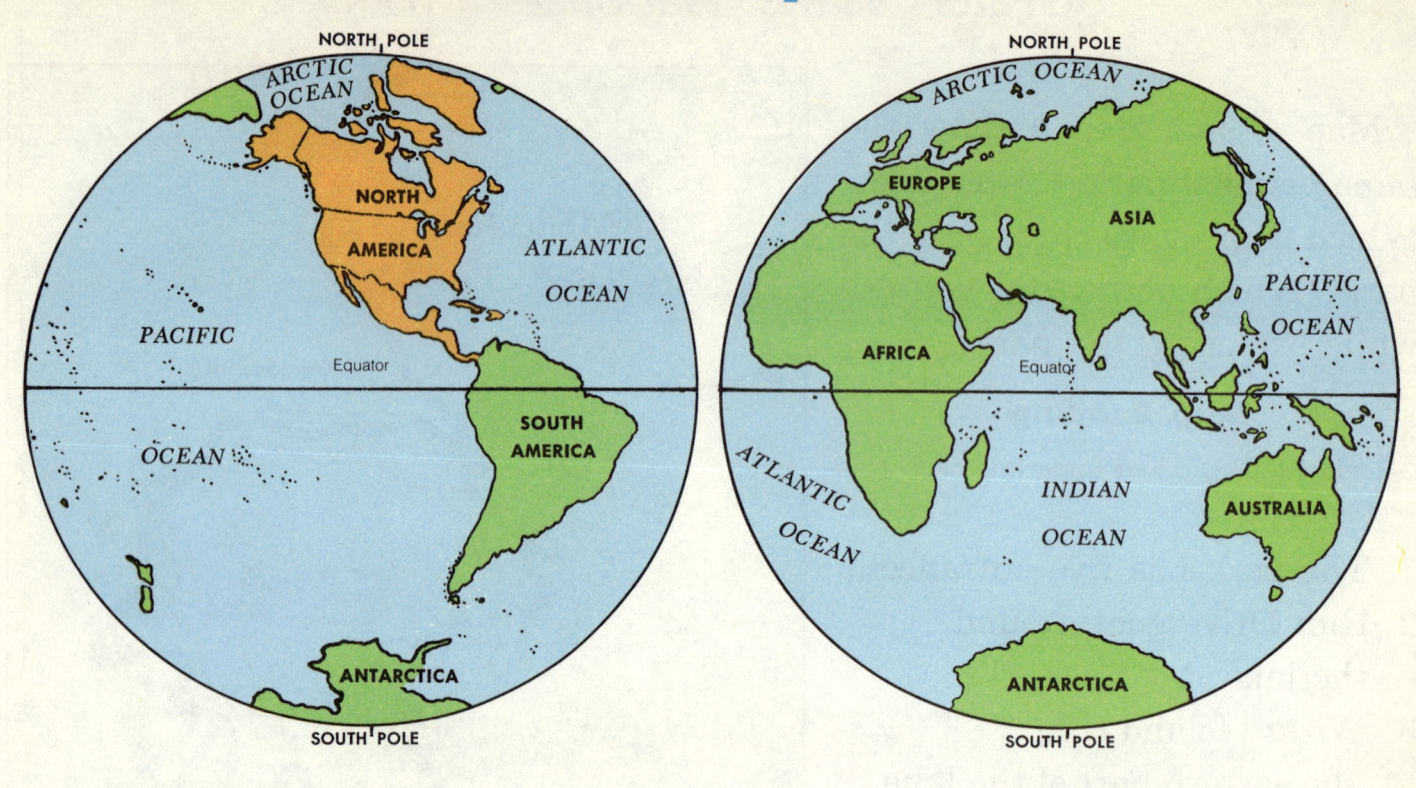

Dear Mapmaker,

I am puzzled. I found a line on my globe. The line goes around the middle of the globe. I found the same line on the globe pictures that I am sending. What does the line mean?

Yours truly,

Tommy Trip

Dear Tommy,

The line you found is called the *equator*. It is a line drawn halfway between the North Pole and the South Pole. The equator divides the globe into two equal parts.

Yours truly,

Mapmaker

Using the Maps

Underline each true sentence.

1. The equator crosses land and water.
2. The equator is nearer to the South Pole than to the North Pole.
3. The equator crosses North America.
4. The equator is halfway between the North Pole and the South Pole.

Circle the continent name that *best* completes each sentence.

1. South of the equator is ....
   Australia   Europe   North America
2. Nearest to the South Pole is ....
   Africa   Asia   Antarctica
3. North of the equator is ....
   Antarctica   Australia
   North America
4. The equator crosses ....
   Africa   Europe   Antarctica

North America

NORTH — **SOUTH** — **WEST** — **EAST**

ARCTIC OCEAN • GREENLAND • UNITED STATES • CANADA • Great Lakes • UNITED STATES • PACIFIC OCEAN • ATLANTIC OCEAN • MEXICO

Tommy takes another look at North America.

What new things does he see?

Studying North America

Underline each true sentence.

1. Greenland is the largest island.
2. A boundary line crosses the Great Lakes.
3. The map shows cities in the U.S.
4. Mexico has mountains in the west.
5. Mexico is larger than Canada.
6. The Arctic Ocean is nearer to Mexico than to Canada.

Use these words to complete the sentences: *northern, southern, western, eastern.*

1. Most of the mountains are in the _____ part of the U.S.
2. Many islands are found in the _____ part of Canada.
3. The Atlantic Ocean touches the _____ side of the U.S.
4. Mexico is in the _____ part of North America.

… The United States has 50 states. Forty-eight are connected. Which two states are not connected to the others?

The United States

Size and Direction

Circle the word or group of words that *best* completes each sentence.

1. Of the 48 connected states, the largest is ....
   Wyoming   Texas   Florida

2. Arizona is .... of Utah.
   east   north   south

3. Colorado is .... of Kansas.
   south   west   east

4. Maine is smaller than ....
   Vermont   Montana   Connecticut

5. Kansas is larger than ....
   Iowa   Colorado   Wyoming

6. South of Arizona is ....
   California   Utah   Mexico

Map Study

Circle the word or group of words that *best* completes each sentence.

1. A group of islands make up the state of ....
   Utah   Hawaii   Maine

2. The Columbia River forms the boundary of Washington and ....
   Oregon   Idaho   Arizona

3. The state of Michigan is divided into two parts by ....
   a river   a lake   an ocean

4. The state which borders both the Arctic Ocean and the Pacific Ocean is ....
   Virginia   California   Alaska

Map Skills Review—Symbols and Directions

A.
B.
C.
D.
E.
F.
G.
H.
I.

Map Symbols

Finish each sentence by writing the correct letter or letters in the blank.

1. The symbol for a railroad is _____.
2. The symbol for a lake is _____.
3. The symbol for mountains is _____.
4. The symbol for a bridge is _____.
5. The symbol for hills is _____.
6. The symbol for buildings is _____.
7. The symbol for a river is _____.
8. The symbol for a tree is _____.
9. The symbol for roads is _____.

BIG TOWN

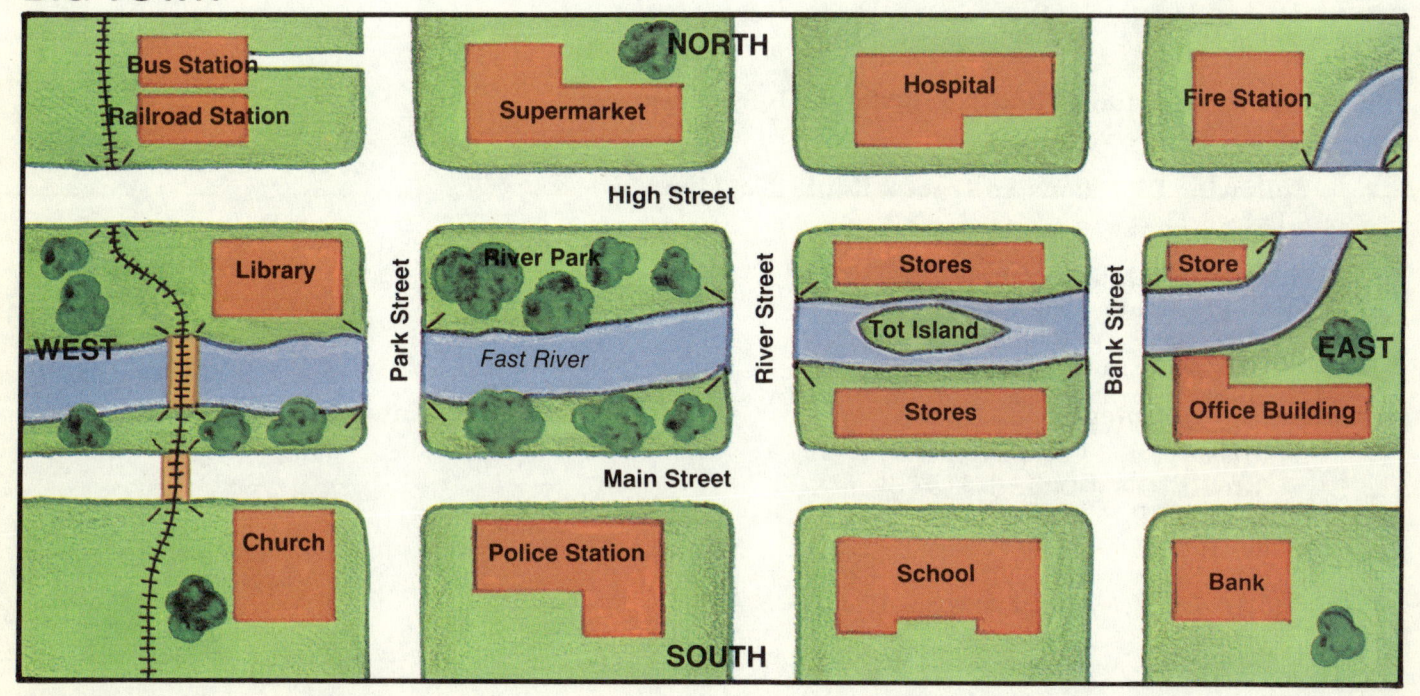

Map Reading

Look at the map of Big Town. Then underline each true sentence.

1. There are five bridges over Fast River.
2. The police station is north of River Street.
3. Buildings are shown on Tot Island.
4. A railroad runs through Big Town.
5. A railroad bridge runs over Main Street.
6. The school is south of the fire station.
7. There are trees in River Park.
8. To get from the bus station to the bank, you must go south and west.

Index of Skills and Understandings

Understanding the Globe
Introduction: pages 3, 4

Understanding Maps
Introduction: page 4, 5
Relating photos to maps: pages 5–7, 9, 10

Determining Positions on Maps and Globes
Using relative location: pages 10–16, 20, 22, 24–30
Using cardinal directions: pages 17–31
Using the Equator: page 28

Determining Distances and Sizes
Using relative distance: pages 10, 14, 16, 19–22, 24–29
Using relative size: pages 7, 10, 12–16, 19, 20, 22, 24–26, 29, 30

Determining Directions
Using the North and South poles: pages 3, 28
Using directions—north, south, east, west: pages 17–22, 25, 26

Comparing Maps, Photos, and Making Inferences
Pages 6, 9, 12, 15, 16, 21, 27

Following Directions To Trace a Route on a Map
Pages 8, 17, 25

Recognizing Map Symbols
Introduction: pages 4–6, 9, 10
Landforms
  Continents: pages 3–5, 28, 29
  Mountains: pages 9, 13, 16, 19, 20, 24–26, 29, 31
  Hills: pages 9, 11, 13, 16, 29, 20, 24–27, 31
  Island: pages 10–13, 16, 22, 24–27, 29–31
  Trees, forests: pages 7–15, 17, 23, 25, 31

Water forms
  Oceans: pages 3–5, 10, 11, 24, 26, 28–30
  Rivers, creeks, brooks: pages 5, 7, 9–12, 15, 19, 22–24, 26, 27, 30, 31
  Lakes, ponds: pages 5, 7, 8, 12–14, 16–19, 23–27, 29–31

Man-made features
  Streets, roads: pages 6–8, 11–15, 18–27, 31
  Bridges: pages 6–10, 12–14, 22, 24–26, 31
  Buildings: pages 7–11, 13–15, 19–22, 24–27, 31
  Boundary lines: pages 15, 23, 29, 30
  Cities: pages 15, 16, 20, 21, 24, 26, 27, 29
  Railroads: pages 9–11, 19, 24, 26, 31

Photograph Credits: Page 5, Harold M. Lambert Studios, Inc., David W. Hamilton for The Image Bank (top to bottom); p. 6, Wendler for The Image Bank, Joe Azzara for The Image Bank (top to bottom); p. 7, Joe Azzara for Frederic Lewis, Inc.; p. 9, Frank "Shorty" Wilcox for The Image Bank, Robert Koropp for The Image Bank (top to bottom); p. 10, Michael DeCamp for The Image Bank.